IRISH
COUNTRY LIFE

To Mam —
Remembrance of trip to Ireland
in 1998 – June 7th — June 29th.
Love Emer.

IRISH
COUNTRY
LIFE

PARKGATE
BOOKS

First Published in Great Britain in 1997
by Parkgate Books Ltd, London House, Great Eastern Wharf,
London SW11 4NQ

All photographs © Hulton Getty Picture Collection,
Unique House, 21-31 Woodfield Road, London W9 2BA.
Tel 0171 266 2660, Fax 0171 266 2414

British Library Cataloguing in Publication Data:
A CIP catalogue record for this book is available from the
British Library.

ISBN 1-85585-309-4

Compiled by Philippa Lewis
Designed by Bill Mason
Printed and bound in Great Britain by
Butler & Tanner Ltd, Frome and London

INTRODUCTION

These photographs of an Ireland past were taken in the years between the end of
the 19th century and the middle of the 20th. They illustrate some of the aspects
beloved of Ireland's own people and of visitors to the Emerald Isle.

The pictures dating from the 1880s correspond to a period of pride and
curiosity in Ireland's rich heritage, in its history and culture. It was during this
time that its folklore, and fast-disappearing customs and pastimes, were
revived and recorded for future generations. The re-introduction by the Gaelic
Athletic Association in 1884 of the sport of hurling, and the encouragement by
the Gaelic League, founded in 1893, of the use of the old language of Ireland,
are but two examples of this interest in the past.

Time marches on, though, and many of the photographs are of a world that can
never be recaptured.

CELTIC IRELAND

Celtic crosses as part of the everyday landscape, a symbol of the Christianity brought to Ireland in the 5th century by St Patrick and quickly accepted by the Irish kings in place of their earlier pagan worship. The ancient cross standing in the town of Kells, Co. Meath (above), was moved from the graveyard and served as a market cross; during the 18th century it was used as a gallows, which may account for its broken top.

TULLY CROSS, DUBLIN.

6

DUNLUCE CASTLE, 4016. W.L.

THE EMERALD ISLE

Ireland has always been famed for its extraordinary natural beauty. A caravanner winds his way along the unmade roads of Connemara between lake and mountains. Tourists of an earlier date view Dunluce Castle on the Antrim coast from the first electric tramway in Ireland. The castle was the main stronghold of the Mac Donnells, Lords of the Isles. It was built on a crag cut off from the mainland at high tide, when it was accessible from the sea only by way of a cave with a stair that led up through the rock.

IRISH CHILDREN

*Happy, barefooted and carefree: children
playing in front of their cottage in Galway Bay.
Two schoolboys standing in the distinctive
limestone landscape of the Aran Islands*

TRADITIONAL COTTAGES

The traditional single-storey thatched cottage, once to be seen everywhere but now vanishing from the Irish landscape. In 1841 nearly half the houses were one-roomed cabins. Most were built of stone, but in some areas they were of mud or sod, or in rare cases of brick. Straw was the usual thatching material, but rushes and river or lake reeds were common in some places, as was flax; potato stalks, heather and bracken were also known to have been used. Along the western coasts, battered by strong south-westerly winds, the thatch was kept in place by a network of hay-ropes weighted down with stones. The cow byre was sometimes built under the same roof as the dwelling, providing a little extra warmth.

HEARTH AND HOME

*All the business of life took place about the hearth. One
19th-century writer described a cottage with 'a few lighted
sods of turf which, while they afford but a little warmth to
the wretched group around them, fill the room with
volumes of smoke'. These pictures belie that description.
Inside the Donegal cottage (right) is the traditional
recessed bed beside the fire. The peaceful Aran Island
interior (above) has implements showing how the hearth
was used for cooking.*

14

STORYTELLING

*Keeping alive the Irish folk tradition
as late as 1947, when these
photographs were taken. The villagers
of Teelin in Co. Donegal gather
round to listen to the old man.
Stories were told by the fireside on
long winter evenings, beginning with
the man of the house and ending with
tales told by neighbours and any
traveller passing through, be he
craftsman or beggar. Among the
stories were the ancient Celtic myths,
with Cú Chulainn and Fionn Mac
Cumhaill as the heroes and the
beautiful Deidre as the heroine.
The stories, originally in Gaelic,
survived translation into the
English language.*

IRISH AIRS

*A piper playing the traditional Uileann pipes at the Ould
Lammas Fair held at the end of August in Ballycastle, Co.
Antrim. The Irish bagpipes are pumped with the piper's elbow so
that he may sing as his plays. The song about the fair goes:*

> *'Did you treat your Mary-Ann
> To dulse and yellow man
> At the Ould Lammas Fair in Ballycastle.'*

*On July 12th it is the turn of the fife and the huge Lambeg drum
to be heard, commemorating the victory of William of Orange
over James II at the Battle of the Boyne.*

PUTTING TO SEA

The importance of boats to an island people: the curragh (below and top left), the traditional boat for west-coast islanders, photographed here in calm water though capable of riding the fierce Atlantic seas. The writer J. M. Synge, who spent a year on the Aran Islands, described travelling in a curragh: 'The sail is only used as an aid, so the men continued to row after it had gone up, and as they occupied the four cross-seats I lay on the canvas at the stern on the frame of slender laths, which bent and quivered as the waves passed under them.' Supplies, mail, livestock and passengers from the mainland to the Aran Islands were for many years carried by the steamer Dun Aengus, *which on Tuesdays and Saturdays plied the 30 miles to and from Inishmore.*

SHIPBUILDING

The yard of the shipbuilders Harland and Wolff, one of the most famous in the British Isles, where many great ships, including the Titanic, *were built. Belfast's geographical position made it a natural place for building ships, the lough being a natural haven and the forests around the mouth of the Lagan supplying the timber. The firm was founded when Edward Harland and Gustav Wolff joined forces in 1861, and together they revolutionized many aspects of the industry.*
These photographs show the keel of the Olympic *being laid in 1911, and the workforce emerging from the yard at about the same date.*

H A R V E S T I N G   T H E   S E A S

The rich fishing-grounds around Ireland were legendary,
and all around the coast the harvest from the sea provided
a livelihood for many families. The fishing fleet returned
to harbour at Ardglass, Co. Down, in 1935 (above).
The glut of herrings in the 1930s meant that the catch
sometimes had to be dumped back in the sea.
Fishermen on the island of Inishmore (right)
carry their nets across the rocks.

COLLECTING SEAWEED

*Winkles, cockles, mussels, crab and crayfish were spoils
from the sea, and also seaweed. Seaweed, or kelp, was
collected from the beach in baskets at low tide or else cut
from boats using knives on long poles. It was used as a
fertilizer on the potato fields or piled up in large ricks
before being burned in kilns along the shore. When cooled,
the calcined ash was sold for the extraction of iodine.
These pictures show seaweed gatherers (above) near
Fairhead in Co. Antrim, and Aran islanders bringing
their load up from the beach (left).*

SEASIDE PLEASURES

Scenes at Bray, Co. Wicklow, one of the first coastal resorts in Ireland. Sedate Victorians on the promenade shield themselves from the sun with parasols (right), and their descendants, photographed 50 years later, sit happily on the beach (above). Bray has always been a popular resort for Dubliners, and Oscar Wilde spent holidays there in his childhood.

THE ISLANDERS

A group photograph of the dwellers on Aranmore dating from the turn of the century is captioned 'The Descendants of Firbolgs'. The legend is that the Firbolgs, small and dark-skinned, were defeated in battle by the contrastingly fair and tall Tuatha dé Danann, in a fight lasting five days, and driven out to the islands and to infertile land by the sea. Wearing traditional jersey, knitted bobble hat and tweed trousers, an Aran islander makes pampooties — tough hide moccasins that were ideal for walking over sharp rocks and on slippery seaweed. They were kept wet with sea water to stop them becoming painfully hard on the feet. The Donegal and Aran jerseys were originally knitted by men, using undyed wool. Distinctive patterns and stitches were supposed to enable a family to identify their menfolk who had been shipwrecked. For women the traditional dress was a long red woollen skirt, black-laced top and shawl.

THE BIG HOUSE

*One of the most remarkable features of Ireland is the
number and size of the houses built by families, originally
from England, who settled in Ireland from Tudor times
onwards. Many have the appellation 'Castle', and the first
Anglo-Irish certainly lived in semi-fortified houses; by the
Georgian period, though, the castellation on the buildings
was strictly ornamental. In the 20th century the vast scale
of some of the houses made them almost impossible to
maintain. The Viceroy, his family and staff outside
the Vice-Regal Lodge in Phoenix Park, Dublin, in the
1860s (right). Renamed Aras an Uachtarain,
this is now the home of the Irish President.
Dunsany Castle, Co. Meath (above).*

IRISH CITIES

*Derry, founded on land granted to St Columba, or St
Colmcille, by Aimire, Prince of the O'Neills, in 546. It is
the most complete walled city in Ireland and is encircled
by early 17th-century walls. An early 20th-century view of
Ferryquay Gate (below left), one of the seven city gates.
Cork, Ireland's second city, situated on the River Lee. A
view of The Mall in the 1880s (above left), and a quieter
view of the quays (above) in the mid-20th century.*

HORSES

Horses were of the greatest importance and interest to most Irishmen. In Co. Kerry hard bargaining takes place at the door (left), with a potential buyer, offered a horse by a traveller, checking the age of the horse by inspecting its teeth. A blacksmith, one of the most valued men in the community, outside his forge (above).

HORSE-DRAWN TRAFFIC

A traveller to Ireland in 1834 wrote: 'Although there are carriages of all descriptions in Ireland and coaches too, the jaunting car is the national vehicle and Ireland would scarcely be Ireland without it. It may be said to completely supersede as a private vehicle the whole of the gig tribe — dennet, tilbury, cariolet etc.' Jaunting cars were two wheeled and lightweight, and passengers would sit sideways with their feet dangling. The street scene photographed in 1945 shows jaunting cars loaded with racegoers on the way to Galway Races, in vehicles very like the ones of a century before.

TRAVELLERS

A travelling family in Co. Clare photographed in 1950 in a traditional roll-top caravan. The travellers took to the road between seasonal jobs and fairs, trading horses, ponies and donkeys as they went on their way. In the 19th century the traveller was often an itinerant tinsmith, or tinker, making and mending tinwares of all shapes and sizes for farms and cottages.

FARMERS

Agriculture was always the backbone of Ireland's economy, with a great many people depending on the family farm for their livelihood. Harvesting (left) on the rolling farmland near Ballynahinch, Co. Down. Ploughing (above) at Murlough Bay on the Antrim coast; Fair Head, one of the northernmost points of Ireland is in the distance.

DAIRY FARMING

*An old woman in Donegal keeps watch over her cows grazing
close to the shore. On a small farm of about 30 acres only six or
seven cows could be kept. The cream would be sold and the
separated milk fed to the pigs, along with a small amount of
home-produced grain. Some farmers would have had to deliver
their milk to the creamery, but this farmer in Co. Fermanagh
put his churn in the lane for the creamery lorry to collect.
The thatched roof of the stand kept the sun off the milk and
prevented it turning.*

THE MARKET PLACE

Farmers gather round the market cross in Tuam, Co. Galway, to sell their potatoes, the staple food of the Irish. Describing how the Aran islanders sustained themselves, J. M. Synge wrote: 'They seem to eat together in the evening, and sometimes in the morning, a little after dawn, but during the day they simply drink a cup of tea and eat a piece of bread, or some potatoes, whenever they are hungry.'

WOMEN'S SHAWLS

The most distinctive garment worn by Irish women, the shawl. It was usually large enough to cover the head and much of the body, and could be used, as in the photograph taken in Galway market in 1935 (left), to hide from the camera. The bright patterns can be seen more clearly on women's shawls at a pony fair at Carna, Co. Galway (below).

COLLEENS

Irish girls photographed in the 1950s. Two girls in their traditional shawls against a Galway landscape contrasted with two girls walking for the last time near Kilternan, Co. Dublin, before they emigrated to England. At that time some 20,000 young Irish men and women left Ireland each year in search of work.

THE CATHOLIC CHURCH

*The faithful flock to mass at Cross Chapel, Greenane, Co.
Kerry, in May 1925. Seminarians stroll in front of the
enormous Gothic Revival seminary at Armagh, or stay
indoors and attend to their religious studies.*

HOLY PLACES

*A Capuchin monk blesses the rosary of a young boy
making the pilgrimage to Croagh Patrick in Co. Mayo
(right), the sacred and beautiful mountain where St
Patrick is believed to have fasted and prayed for the 40
days and 40 nights of Lent in the year 441. A wayside
shrine in Dublin (above), photographed during
the Second World War.*

THE RACES

Scenes at Galway Races photographed in 1945. The races last for a week in early August and crowds, including priests among the farmers, gather there from all over the country. Some have their year's savings in their pockets, to be spent on bets, and serious drinking as well. The highlight of the meeting is the Galway Plate.

PLACING A BET

The Irish passion for betting means that betting shops are to be found everywhere. This one (above) was photographed in Dublin. A bookie on the racecourse (left) takes bets for the Leopardstown Chase in 1949, and a more informal bet is laid between two bystanders at a road-bowling match (right).

ROAD BOWLING

A game unique to Ireland, played on quiet, winding roads. An iron ball, or 'bullet', is thrown along the lane, with the aim of covering a set distance in the fewest number of throws. Money changes hands in bets among the spectators before the competition. Young lads playing the game are pictured here.

HURLING

*Scenes at the semi-final of the Irish Hurling Cup in 1950,
when Tipperary beat Galway by 19 points to 12. There
are 15 players a side, each armed with a hurley — a
metre of solid ash with a flattened curving blade —
with which to strike a small white leather ball, or 'slitter',
through the goal-mouth. Skilful and dangerous, hurling is
very exciting for the spectators. A craftsman makes
hurling balls (right): a core of cork is wrapped in wool,
then covered with thick leather and sewn by hand.*

POTEEN

Home-brewed and illegal: the attractions of poteen, the whiskey made very economically from the ubiquitous potato. In the early photograph (above), children in Connemara cluster round the still; in the later photograph (right), the covert operation is described — with discretion — as taking place 'in a remote part of Ireland'. J. M. Synge, in the Aran Islands, wrote that 'grey poteen, which brings a shock of joy to the blood, seems predestined to keep sanity in men who live forgotten in these worlds of mists'.

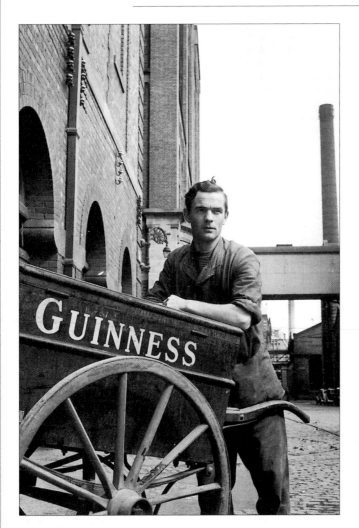

IRELAND'S NATIONAL DRINK

The Guinness brewery at St James's Gate on the banks of the Liffey in Dublin, photographed in the early 1950s. Guinness was first brewed there in 1759, when Arthur Guinness took over an old brewery and began to brew ale and a dark porter that had been invented in London about 30 years earlier. By 1799 his porter was such a success that he stopped brewing ale altogether. A barrow used to take malt samples from one part of the brewery to another (above). An old man making pads onto which the casks fell when they were being moved about (right). A cask being finished by 'blazing' (far right).

DUBLIN BARS

The exterior of O'Meara's Irish House at Wood Quay, Dublin, photographed when it was under threat of demolition. Legend has it that the sculptures on the exterior were made in return for drink by a bibulous and impecunious sculptor. They depict such figures as Henry Grattan, the famous orator. Photographed in the interior of a Dublin bar is the writer Brendan Behan, a legendary figure in the 1950s.

OLD BELFAST

*Belfast at the turn of the century, a view down the High
Street to the Albert Memorial clock (above). The wealth
and importance of 19th-century Belfast is demonstrated by
its grand Victorian buildings. In 1759 the population was
only 8,549, and the streets were dark and dirty. The port,
the linen industry and shipbuilding were the foundations
on which the city grew to prosperity. The Orange Hall
(left), from which the July 12th processions set out, which
bears the date 1690 of the Battle of the Boyne.*

OLD DUBLIN

*A historic view of O'Connell Street in Dublin. Formerly
called Sackville Street, it was renamed in 1927 for Daniel
O'Connell, the lawyer who won Catholic Emancipation.
On the left is the General Post Office, where the Irish
Republic was declared and the Volunteers held off
government forces for a week following the Easter Rising
in 1916. Trams continued to run until the 1950s; the
monument to Nelson was blown up in 1966. A vignette of
Edwardian Dublin: a tobacconist's shop front.*

GEORGIAN DUBLIN

*The Customs House on the north
bank of the Liffey, designed by the
architect James Gandon and
completed in 1791. One of the
grandest Georgian buildings in
Dublin, it was photographed here at
the end of the 19th century, when
Dublin still had a thriving port,*

THE DUBLIN HORSE SHOW

*The biggest social event in the Irish calendar, with judging
and events for every class of horse, as well as bloodstock
sales. In 1922 one man's evident enjoyment of the day's
events was caught by the camera (far right), and a
spectator was photographed in her stylish culottes (right).
Thirty years later (below), nothing much had changed.*

THE DONKEY

Tradition has it that donkeys became such a feature of Irish life at the time of the Napoleonic wars, when great numbers of horses were shipped abroad for the army in Europe, but it is more likely that there were donkeys here from the very earliest times. Able to carry heavy loads, they have been much used for carrying turf and seaweed — and of course people. The usual method of a loading a donkey was to sling baskets, or creels, on either side of its back from a wooden pack-saddle, which sat on a pad of woven straw. The saddle was held in place by a rope under the donkey's belly or a crupper under its tail.

PEAT

*The warm, wet climate has given Ireland its
famous bogs, supplying the island with its prime
source of fuel. Peat from the bogs was cut into
bricks and stacked up to dry. The turf was then
taken home to use on the cottage fire.
The smell of peat smoke would be familiar
to any Irish man or woman.*

RIDING TO HOUNDS

*'A horseman's paradise', wrote the hunting correspondent
of 'The Times' of London in 1933. 'Wire is rare and
tarred roads are negligible; indeed, the horses are still
frightened by motor-cars. You may easily hunt the fox
seven days a week, if the local harriers will satisfy you on
Sunday.' The famous Galway Blazers are photographed
with the pack's kennel-men (right). Drinks are served by
footmen at Dunsany Castle at the start of the meet of the
Royal Meath Hunt in 1923 (above).*

DONEGAL TWEED

Photographs taken at the turn of the century in Donegal. A young woman takes the wool out of a three-legged iron cauldron used for dyeing and lays it out to dry (below). A woman spins outside her cottage in Mulroy Bay, near Rosapenna (right). Her spinning wheel would have been one of the family's most valued possessions, the yarn she spun made into the tweed for which the county was famous. Beside her are some baskets, which would have been used for various different purposes inside her cottage — not only for carrying things but as makeshift furniture.

THE WEAVER

While the women spun the wool, the men did the weaving. This Victorian photograph taken in Donegal shows a weaver at work in his cottage (right), where the loom took up almost the whole room. Little has apparently changed for the weaver, as shown by the photograph taken on Aran in the middle of the 20th century (below).

COMING TO TOWN

The farmer shares his van with the two calves he is bringing to market at Mulling Ar, Co. Meath (left), while an old woman in Foynes, Co. Limerick, packs cabbages on the back of a donkey cart (above).

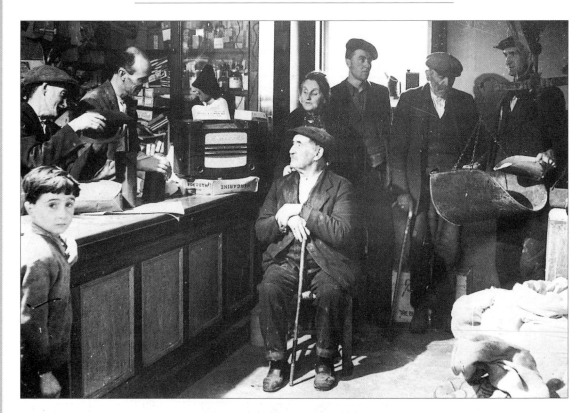

SHOPPING

*The faces of shoppers: an old man in the village of Quin in
Co. Limerick sits down in a shop for a talk in 1940. A
plant-stall attracts attention one morning in a Belfast
street market. A street singer entertains shoppers in a
crowded Dublin street.*

OLD CUSTOMS

*A popular Irish custom took place on the day after Christmas, St Stephen's Day.
Commemorating the death of the wren, king of the birds, on that day, the so-called 'Wren'
boys dressed up in costume and went around the neighbourhood collecting money to bury the
wren. On every doorstep they chanted 'The wren, the wren, King of all the birds, on St
Stephen's day he was caught in the furze'. They took with them a decorated holly branch,
which represented the furze. The money was usually put towards food and drink for the
Wren dance held that evening. In these pictures excited children show the decorated
furze, and rather older Wren boys accept a drink on their rounds.*

FESTIVALS

Singing, dancing and storytelling played an important part in Irish festivities, with festivals appearing regularly on the calendar. The first one of the year was St Brigid's Day, on February 1st. This scene shows a Wren dance on St Stephen's night, at the very end of the year.

THE CHRISTMAS CANDLE

*Keeping up the old custom of lighting a candle in the
window in case the Virgin and Child should pass by
looking for somewhere to stay.*